Democracy

Government in Australia

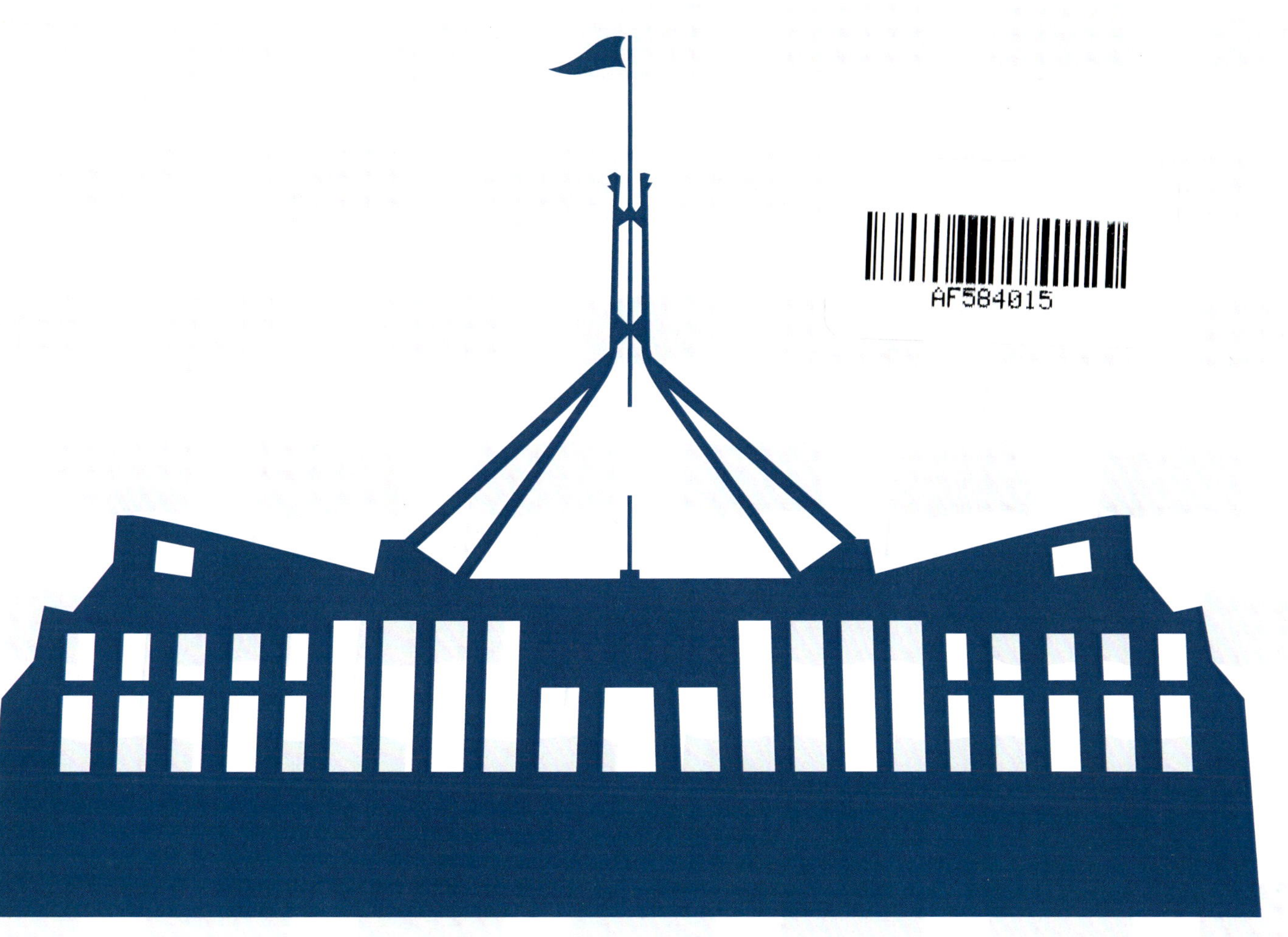

AF584015

Pearson Australia
(a division of Pearson Australia Group Pty Ltd)
707 Collins Street, Melbourne, Victoria 3008
PO Box 23360, Melbourne, Victoria 8012
www.pearson.com.au

Copyright © Pearson Australia 2012
(a division of Pearson Australia Group Pty Ltd)
First published 2011 by Pearson Australia
2015 2014 2013
10 9 8 7 6 5 4 3 2

Reproduction and communication for educational purposes
The Australian *Copyright Act 1968* (the Act) allows a maximum of one chapter or 10% of the pages of this work, whichever is the greater, to be reproduced and/or communicated by any educational institution for its educational purposes provided that that educational institution (or the body that administers it) has given a remuneration notice to Copyright Agency Limited (CAL) under the Act. For details of the CAL licence for educational institutions contact Copyright Agency Limited (www.copyright.com.au).

Reproduction and communication for other purposes
Except as permitted under the Act (for example any fair dealing for the purposes of study, research, criticism or review), no part of this book may be reproduced, stored in a retrieval system, communicated or transmitted in any form or by any means without prior written permission. All enquiries should be made to the publisher at the address above.

This book is not to be treated as a blackline master; that is, any photocopying beyond fair dealing requires prior written permission.

PHOTOCOPYING OF BOOKS IS RESTRICTED UNDER LAW

Authors: Andrew Einspruch and Cameron Macintosh
Publisher: Sarah Russell
Project Editor: Rachel Davis
Editor: Writers Reign
Designers: Anne Donald, Jan Urbanic and Kim Ferguson
Cover Designer: Glen McClay
Copyright & Pictures Editor: Katy Murenu
Printed and bound in Australia by Pegasus Media & Logistics

National Library of Australia Cataloguing-in-Publication entry
Author: Einspruch, Andrew.
Title: Government in Australia / Cameron Macintosh and Andrew Einspruch.
ISBN: 9781442559691 (pbk.)
Series: Democracy.
Notes: Includes index.
Target Audience: For primary school age.
Subjects: Political science--Australia--Juvenile literature.
Australia--Politics and government--Juvenile literature.
Other Authors/Contributors: Macintosh, Cameron.
Dewey Number: 320.994

Pearson Australia Group Pty Ltd ABN 40 004 245 943

Acknowledgements
We would like to thank the following for permission to reproduce copyright material.
The following abbreviations are used in this list: t = top, b = bottom.

AAP: pp. 9b, 21b; David Crosling, p. 21t; Mark Graham, p. 11b; Patrick Hamilton, p. 29b; Julian Smith, p. 17.
Alamy: p. 22.
Commonwealth of Australia: © 2011, p. 12.
Corbis: David Ashley, p. 6; Richard Hutchings, p. 5t.
Fairfax Photo Sales: p. 16; Michael Clayton-Jones, p. 24.
Getty Images: p.27; Matt King, p. 18.
High Court of Australia: p. 11t.
Lonely Planet Images: John Hay, p. 14; Oliver Strewe, p. 26.
National Archives of Australia: p. 9t.
Newspix: Richard Gosling, p. 5b; Leigh Winburn, p. 29t.
Shutterstock: cover.

Every effort has been made to trace and acknowledge copyright. However, if any infringement has occurred, the publishers tender their apologies and invite the copyright holders to contact them.

Disclaimer/s
The selection of Internet addresses (URLs) provided for this book was valid at the time of publication and was chosen as being appropriate for use as a primary education research tool. However, due to the dynamic nature of the Internet, some addresses may have changed, may have ceased to exist since publication, or may inadvertently link to sites with content that could be considered offensive or inappropriate. While the authors and publisher regret any inconvenience this may cause readers, no responsibility for any such changes or unforeseeable errors can be accepted by either the authors or the publisher.

Some of the images used in *Democracy: Government in Australia* might have associations with deceased Indigenous Australians. Please be aware that these images might cause sadness or distress in Aboriginal or Torres Strait Islander communities.

Contents

Words that are printed in bold are explained in the Glossary on page 31.

What Is Democracy?

Democracy is a way of making group decisions that allows everyone in the group to have a say. It is a system that tries to work out what is best for the whole group while keeping in mind the rights of the individuals within it. The word 'democracy' comes from the ancient Greeks, and it means the 'rule of the people' or 'majority rule'. Abraham Lincoln, the 16th president of the United States, described democracy as 'government of the people, by the people, for the people'.

Democracy: Key Beliefs

- Individuals within a group are equal and no one is better or has a higher value than anyone else.
- The things that happen to a group affect all its members.
- The best decisions for a group are those that everyone has discussed and understood.
- Every individual within a group needs to feel safe and be protected.

Forms of Democracy

There are two main forms of democracy—direct democracy and indirect democracy.

Direct Democracy

In a direct democracy, people can have a say in decision-making by voicing their opinions or voting directly on any issues that might affect them. Direct democracy works best in small groups and communities where it is easy for everyone to get information or to voice an opinion. In larger communities, this becomes too difficult. There are often hundreds of issues that need to be discussed, and it is impossible for each person to know enough about every issue to make an informed decision.

Indirect Democracy

In an indirect democracy, commonly called a **representative** democracy, certain people are elected by members of the community to represent them in an **assembly** or **parliament**. These representatives make decisions on behalf of the people who voted for them. Because of their size, modern democratic nations are nearly always representative democracies.

Protecting Democracy

In order for a democracy to be truly representative, it is important to ensure that there are safeguards to stop the government from becoming too powerful, and to guarantee that people's rights and freedoms are protected. Some of the safeguards in a representative democracy include a written **constitution**, fair laws that can be upheld by an independent legal system, freedom of speech, a free media and access to government information.

About This Book

This book looks at the role and operation of government in the Australian democracy. It explores the operation and structure of government at federal, state and local levels, and details the roles of various government departments. The book also looks at ways in which Australians outside the government can work to persuade their leaders to act on particular issues.

These students are voting for a class leader, which shows democracy in action at school.

These workers are meeting to discuss improving their work conditions, which shows democracy in action.

Australia's Government

A government is a group of leaders who make decisions about how a society runs. To do this, governments make laws—rules that people must follow. They also make **policies**, which are guidelines or plans for what the government wants to do in particular areas such as defence, health or transport. Good governments make decisions that they feel benefit the people the most and, as much as possible, reflect what the majority of people want.

Government Services

People need many different services, such as schools, hospitals, rubbish collection, police to help keep order, and emergency services. They want national parks, courts of law and public transport. Our society works together to provide these things for everyone's benefit. We choose representatives to form governments that make these types of decisions for us.

Different Types of Government

Different countries have different types of governments. Not all of them are chosen by the people. For example, in a **military junta**, the **armed forces** take power by force and military officers make the government's decisions. In a **dictatorship**, one person (usually backed by the armed forces) has absolute power and makes decisions without being limited by laws. If religious leaders are in charge, the government is called a **theocracy**.

Australia is a **democracy**. In democracies, people vote in elections to choose their representatives. Regular elections give people the chance to choose new representatives.

Who Does What?

There are three levels of government in Australia: federal, state and territory, and local. The federal government makes decisions that affect the whole country. State and territory governments make decisions that affect their particular state or territory. Local governments take responsibility for small areas within a state.

Schools are the responsibility of state and territory governments.

Levels of Government in Australia

Type of Government	How Many Are There?	Makes Decisions About …
Federal	1	National matters: • defence • **immigration** and **citizenship** • money and banking • relationships with other countries • environment • telecommunications • welfare payments and other types of **financial** assistance • higher education • public health (including Medicare) • protecting the environment
State and territory	6 state 2 territory	State matters: • hospitals • police and emergency services • public housing • business regulation • schools • state roads
Local	565 (as of 2011)	Local issues: • community services, such as child care and aged care • libraries • local planning and development • local roads, bridges and footpaths • recreation facilities, such as pools and parks • waste management • water and **sewerage** services

Australia's Constitutions

A **constitution** is a written set of principles and laws that describe a government's powers and duties. A constitution sets the ground rules for government. The Constitution of Australia guides the federal government, while state governments work within the limits set by their own constitutions.

Australia's Federal Constitution

The Constitution of the Commonwealth of Australia came into effect on 1 January 1901. Before this, Australia was made up of a collection of separate British colonies, each of which ruled itself. The new constitution created a **commonwealth**, changing the colonies into Australian states with a federal government in place above them.

The Constitution is specific about what the federal government can do. It states that the government can 'make laws for the peace, order and good government of the Commonwealth', then lists what those laws can cover. Some of these responsibilities are listed in the chart on page 7. Other responsibilities include:

- lighthouses
- the postal system
- **quarantine**
- marriage and divorce
- trade with other countries.

Any area not covered by the Constitution is the responsibility of the states. However, if a state law says one thing and a federal law says something different, the federal law must be followed.

State Constitutions

State constitutions existed before there was a federal one, because before 1901 the colonies governed themselves. The states of Victoria, New South Wales and Tasmania were established first, with constitutions passed in 1855. A state constitution describes how the state government is set up, what powers it has, how the state constitution can be changed and how long politicians serve once elected.

Territories

Australia controls 10 territories, eight of which are offshore. These include the Australian Antarctic Territory, the Coral Sea Islands and Christmas Island. No territory has a constitution. However, three territories have their own governments: the Australian Capital Territory, the Northern Territory and Norfolk Island. In practice, the Australian Capital Territory and Northern Territory are treated like states.

Difference between States and Territories

	State	Territory
Does it have a constitution?	✓	✗
Was it once an independent colony?	✓	✗
Was it created by a law passed by the federal government?	✗	✓
Can the federal government override its laws?	✗	✓

Making Changes to the Federal Constitution

Australia's Constitution can be changed but the process is complicated. To change any part of the Constitution, the following steps must be followed.

1 The federal government must vote to ask the Australian people for change.

2 The **Governor-General** must put the question to voters.

3 A 'double majority' of voters must approve the change before it can become part of the Constitution. This means a majority of voters across the country and a majority of voters in at least four of the six states need to approve the change.

Commonwealth of Australia Constitution Act.

AN ACT

TO

Constitute the Commonwealth of Australia.

Cap. 12 [9th July 1900]

The original Constitution of the Commonwealth of Australia is held at the National Archives in Canberra. It was originally an Act of the British Parliament, so it was held by the National Archives in the UK until 1988, when it was lent to Australia. In 1990, the British Government gave it to the Australian people as a gift.

Australians voted in a referendum to change the Constitution in 1999 to make Australia a republic. The 'no' vote was victorious. Since 1906, only eight changes to the Constitution have been passed from 43 attempts.

Structure of the Federal Government

There are three branches that make up the federal government. The first is called the **legislature** or **parliament**, which makes Australia's laws. Australia's federal parliament is made up of two groups of elected officials: the House of Representatives and the Senate. The other two branches of the federal government are the **executive**, which runs the government and puts the laws into action, and the **judiciary**, which **interprets** the laws and makes sure that they are followed.

Two Houses

Australia has a **bicameral** system of government. 'Bicameral' refers to the government's two houses (also called 'chambers'). Australia's bicameral federal legislature is made up of the House of Representatives (the Lower House) and the Senate (the Upper House).

House of Representatives

The House of Representatives is made up of 150 members of parliament. Each member represents approximately the same number of people from their state or territory. The population of each state or territory is divided into roughly equal pieces, called **electorates**, and each electorate votes for one representative in the House. The more people a state or territory has, the more representatives it elects.

How Many People in an Electorate?

The number of people in an electorate is around 94 000 on average, although the figure varies from electorate to electorate.

Senate

The states are represented equally in the Senate, with 12 senators from each. The ACT and Northern Territory add two more senators each, bringing the total to 76. Every voter in a state or territory votes for the same candidates for the Senate. The **Constitution** says the Senate should be around half the size of the House of Representatives.

Both houses must pass every proposed law (also called 'bills') for them to take effect, and any member or senator can introduce a bill. The exceptions are **money bills**, which must come from the House of Representatives.

Three Branches

The House of Representatives and the Senate form the legislature, which makes laws. The party that has the most members in the House of Representatives takes control of the government's executive branch. The executive makes sure existing laws are put into practice and guides the government's day-to-day decisions.

The third branch is the judiciary. This is made up of courts, which make sure that laws are being followed. Because laws cannot cover every possible situation, it is up to the courts to interpret how laws apply when there is a disagreement.

The High Court of Australia is the nation's highest legal authority.

The Senate meets in the Senate Chamber to discuss new laws.

Who Is Australia's Head of State?

In the news, the prime minister is most talked about as Australia's leader, but he or she is not Australia's head of state. The Governor-General always opens Parliament and acts as head of state at ceremonies, but the Governor-General is not the head of state either. In fact, Australia's head of state does not even live in Australia. It is a reflection of Australia's past as a collection of British colonies that the head of state is Queen Elizabeth II. Queen Elizabeth is Queen of Australia as well as Queen of the United Kingdom and Northern Ireland.

Heads of State

A head of state is the chief representative of a nation, who also acts as a symbol of that country. In some countries, like the United Kingdom, this is a king or queen. In others, like the United States and France, it is a president.

Who Is in Charge?

The Queen (or any British **monarch**) leaves the running of the country to elected Australians. The prime minister is in charge of the federal government and is the most important politician in the country.

The **Constitution** says that the Governor-General is the Queen's representative, and he or she acts as head of state for the Queen. Although the Constitution says the Governor-General is the Commander-in-Chief of the Australian Defence Forces and must approve all new laws, in practice it is mostly a **ceremonial** role that involves doing what the government asks.

Governor-General's Powers

The Constitution gives the Governor-General certain powers that are used when there is a problem that affects parliament's ability to work. This might happen, for example, if no political party (or group of parties working together) has a majority that lets them take control of government. In that case, the Governor-General chooses the prime minister from the elected members of the Lower House.

Governor-General Quentin Bryce, Australia's first female Governor-General, swears in Julia Gillard as its first female prime minister in June 2010.

Who's Who in Federal Government

Name of Role	Held by the ...	Facts
Head of State	Queen (or King) of Australia	• Role is only ceremonial • **Monarch** always acts on the advice of the prime minister
Executive	Governor-General of Australia	• Acts as Head of State for the monarch • Appointed by the monarch on advice from the prime minister • Role is mostly ceremonial
Head of Government	Prime Minister of Australia	• Always a member of the House of Representatives from the parties or coalition of parties with most members in the House • In practice, is in charge of the **executive** branch of the government
Parliament	House of Representatives (Lower House)	• Members are called 'Members of the House of Representatives' (MHR); also called 'members' or 'MPs' or 'members of parliament' • There are 150 MPs and each represents about the same number of people from their state or territory, so states with large populations, such as New South Wales, have more MPs than states with small populations, such as Tasmania
	Senate (Upper House)	• Members are called senators; also called 'Members' or 'MPs' or 'Members of Parliament' • There are 76 senators—12 from each state, two from the Australian Capital Territory and two from the Northern Territory

Queen Elizabeth II is Australia's Head of State. She visited Australia in October 2011.

Structure of State Governments

Like federal parliament, each state (with the exception of Queensland) has a **bicameral** system. Each state also has a governor appointed by the British **monarch** and a three-branch government, with a **legislature**, an **executive** and a **judiciary**. Queensland, the Australian Capital Territory and the Northern Territory use a unicameral (single house) system and have no Upper House.

Legislative Assemblies and Houses of Assembly

The Lower House in each state, and the single house in the two territories and Queensland, is called the Legislative Assembly (South Australia and Tasmania use the term 'House of Assembly'). Like federal members of the House of Representatives, most assembly members represent roughly an equal number of people from their state or territory **electorates**.

Members of the Lower and the Upper Houses in each state and territory

State or Territory	Number of Assembly Members	Number of Legislative Council Members
Australian Capital Territory	18	–
New South Wales	93	42
Northern Territory	25	–
Queensland	89	–
South Australia	47	22
Tasmania	25	15
Victoria	88	40
Western Australia	59	36

Legislative Councils

The five states that use a bicameral system call their Upper Houses 'Legislative Councils'. Like the federal Senate, most members of Legislative Councils are elected by voters from across the state.

The Northern Territory's Parliament House is the meeting place of the territory's Legislative Assembly.

Three Branches

Each state and territory has a three-branch system of government. The Assemblies and Councils form the **legislature** and make laws. The premier and ministers of each state run the **executive** branch, which puts laws into action. The **judiciary**, through the courts, makes sure that the state's laws are being followed and **interprets** those laws when needed.

Who's Who in State and Territory Governments

Name of Role	Held by ...			Facts
Head of State	Queen (or King) of Australia			• Monarch always acts on the advice of the premier
Executive	States, Australian Capital Territory, Northern Territory	Australian Capital Territory	Northern Territory	
	Governor	Governor-General of Australia acts when needed	**Administrator**	• Acts as head of state for the monarch • Governors are appointed by the monarch on advice from the premiers • Northern Territory Administrator is appointed by the Governor-General of Australia • Role is mostly **ceremonial**
Head of Government	Premier	Chief Minister		• Always a member of the Legislative Assembly/House of Assembly drawn from the parties or **coalition** of parties who won the election • In practice, is in charge of the executive branch of the government
Parliament	Legislative Assembly (New South Wales, Queensland, Victoria, Western Australia, Australian Capital Territory, Northern Territory) House of Assembly (South Australia, Tasmania)			• Acts as the Lower House for states that use the bicameral system • Acts as only House of Parliament for the two territories (Australian Capital Territory and Northern Territory) and Queensland • Members are called 'Member of the Legislative Assembly' (MLA) or 'Member of the House of Assembly' (MHA)
	Legislative Council (New South Wales, South Australia, Tasmania, Victoria, Western Australia)			• Acts as the Upper House for the states listed • Members are called 'Member of the Legislative Council' (MLC)

Structure of Local Governments

Local government councils are much simpler than state or federal governments. A typical local council is made up of elected councillors, a **mayor**, a general manager and council employees. Because they usually represent fewer people than a state electorate, local councils are in a good position to understand community needs.

Local Councils Are Different

The 565 local councils across Australia come in all shapes and sizes. Brisbane City Council in Queensland takes care of the greatest number of people—around one million. The largest, by size, is the Shire of East Pilbara in Western Australia, which has 8000 people spread over 379 000 square kilometres (an area bigger than the size of Germany).

The smallest council by population is the Murchison Shire Council in Western Australia. It covers 44 000 square kilometres (an area about a fifth the size of Victoria), but only has 112 people. Shire sizes can be small too. Western Australia's Peppermint Grove Shire Council has just 1749 people, all living within 2 square kilometres.

The Australian Capital Territory has no local government. Instead, the territory government takes on local government functions.

Things in Common

Even though they differ in size and population, local councils have a lot in common. Voters in the council area elect councillors. Usually, there are around 10, but there can be as few as five or as many as 15. In some places, voters choose a mayor directly. In others, councillors select someone from among themselves to be mayor.

Communities face all sorts of questions. Should we build a new library? Should we allow more houses to be developed? Can businesses put up more billboards? Local councils make these sorts of decisions, taking into account the ideas and opinions of the community that elected them.

Local councillors discuss community issues at a local council meeting.

Who's Who in Local Government

Name of Role	Held by …	Facts
State or territory Minister for Local Government	Member of parliament appointed to the position by the premier or chief minister	• Oversees local government • Makes sure local governments in the state or territory work well
Head of local government	Mayor	• Runs council meetings and represents the council • Also called 'Lord Mayor', 'Shire President' and 'Warden'
Local government	Local councils	• Elected by voters living in the local area • Called councillors
Main **administrator** for the council	General manager	• Not elected; hired by council to run day-to-day operations, such as hiring employees, working with councillors and managing the council's activities

Local Government around Australia

The general term for an area governed by a local council is a local government area (LGA). In Australia, LGAs can be a:

- city
- district council (country areas in South Australia)
- municipality (older, inner-city areas in New South Wales and some country areas in South Australia)
- regional council (larger country areas in New South Wales)
- shire (country area) in New South Wales, Victoria, Queensland and Western Australia only
- towns (small country town areas in Queensland and Western Australia).

The mayor is the head of local government.

Elections

Australians cast secret votes to choose people to represent them. Different voting methods are used depending on the particular government. The two main voting systems used in Australia are **preferential voting** and **proportional voting**.

Compulsory Voting

Australia is one of the few countries that has **compulsory voting**. If you are **eligible**, you have to sign up with the Australian Electoral Commission (AEC). All eligible voters must participate in federal and state elections. Voting in most local council elections is also **compulsory**.

Preferential Voting

In preferential voting, voters number the candidates on the **ballot** to indicate their order of **preference**. Basically, voters are saying, 'I think this person will do the best job, but if I can't have her, then I will choose this person next', and so on.

There are different types of preferential voting. 'Full preferential' means every candidate on the ballot must be numbered for the vote to count. 'Partial preferential' means only some of the candidates need to be numbered. 'Optional preferential' means voters must show a first choice, but can number others if they want.

Under the preferential system, if a candidate gets more than half the '1' (first choice) votes, they win. If no one gets that many, then the person with the least '1' votes is knocked out and their preferences are given to the other candidates. Counting continues. This goes on until someone has the majority.

Proportional Voting

Proportional voting is used when more than one person is elected from a single **electorate**. This system is mainly used for upper-house elections, such as the Senate, where people are chosen from across a state. In this system, the number of available seats is divided up to reflect how much of the vote the party received. For example, if there are 10 seats available, and Party A received 60 per cent of the votes and Party B got the other 40 per cent, then Party A would win six seats and Party B would win four.

Proportional voting can be combined with preferential voting so that voters can express preferences among the candidates.

First Past the Post

Another voting system that is used in some local council elections is known as 'first past the post'. It is a simple system that says whoever gets the most votes wins, even if they do not receive a majority of votes. For instance, if 40 per cent of people voted for candidate X, 30 per cent for candidate Y and 30 per cent for candidate Z, X wins, even though 60 per cent did not vote for X.

Australia is one of the few countries where voting is compulsory.

Which Voting System Where?

	Lower House	Upper House	Term
Federal	Full preferential	Proportional with full preferential	House of Representatives: elected for three years Senate: elected for six years (territory senators for three years)
Australian Capital Territory	Proportional with optional preferential	–	Elected for four years
New South Wales	Optional preferential	Proportional with partial preferential	Legislative Council: elected for eight years Legislative Assembly: elected for four years
Northern Territory	Full preferential	–	Elected for three years, with the election some time in the fourth year
Queensland	Optional preferential	–	Elected for three years
South Australia	Full preferential	Proportional with full preferential	Legislative Council: elected for eight years Legislative Assembly: elected for four years
Tasmania	Proportional with partial preferential	Partial preferential	Legislative Council: elected for six years Legislative Assembly: elected for four years
Victoria	Full preferential	Proportional with partial preferential	Elected for four years
Western Australia	Full preferential	Proportional	Legislative Council: elected for four years Legislative Assembly: elected for four years

Who Can Vote?

You can enrol to vote if you:

- are 17 but you cannot vote until you are 18 years old or older
- are an Australian citizen, or a British subject who was on a Commonwealth electoral roll on 25 January 1984
- have lived for at least one month at your current address.

Party Politics

Political parties are organisations that bring together people with similar views and values. A political party is saying, 'This is what we believe and this is what we will do if we win power', so their purpose is to win elections and control government.

How Political Parties Work

Political parties are made up of members who join the party and pay a membership fee. People normally join because they believe in what the party stands for and want to support those ideas.

It is not hard to start a new party. There are two main requirements:

- a written **constitution** that states the party's goals
- 500 or more members who can vote and are not members of another party. (If the party has one member who is in federal **parliament**, it does not need 500 members.)

All parties must register with the Australian Electoral Commission (AEC) before they can be included on ballot papers in an election.

Major Parties

Two groups dominate Australian politics. On one side is the Australian Labor Party, the oldest party in existence today and the one that traditionally represents workers' interests. On the other side is the Liberal Party, which often teams with the National Party in a **coalition**. The Liberal Party traditionally supports freedom for businesses, while the National Party works for the interests of farmers and country people.

Minor Parties

Minor political parties are much smaller than major parties. There have been hundreds of them and they tend to come and go. Minor parties often represent people with an interest in a single issue, such as gun control or protecting the environment.

If minor parties get enough votes, they can get into parliament. If the governing party does not have a majority in the Senate, they may need support from minor parties to pass laws. When this happens, the minor parties are said to 'hold the **balance of power**'. The minor parties can demand changes before they agree to pass laws. This situation gives minor parties more influence than they would otherwise have.

Two of the most important minor parties have been the Australian Democrats and the Australian Greens. Both have received enough votes in past elections to win several **seats** in the federal Senate.

Party Names

Starting a new political party? Be careful when choosing its name. AEC rules say the name and its **abbreviation** cannot be:

- more than six words
- obscene
- the same or similar name (or abbreviation) used by an unrelated recognised party
- anything with the words 'Independent Party'.

Party supporters on election day encourage people to vote for their candidates by handing out pamphlets.

Bob Brown is the leader of the Australian Greens, which has at times held the balance of power in the Senate.

Executive

The party or **coalition** with the most members in the House of Representatives (the Lower House) forms government. This means that the successful group takes over the **executive** branch of government and becomes responsible for putting laws into action and the day-to-day running of government. Running the government also lets them put in place promises made during the election. There is an executive branch for the federal government and for every state or territory.

Parts of the Executive

The executive branch of the federal government has three parts:

Prime Minister

The prime minister is the country's top politician. He or she is chosen by the winning party or coalition and always comes from the House of Representatives. In practice, voters know before voting each party's choice for prime minister.

Ministers

Ministers are members of parliament (MPs) who are in charge of a particular area of government, such as education, treasury, defence or immigration. They can come from the House of Representatives or the Senate.

Government Departments

Led by the minister, government departments carry out the programs that deliver government services.

The prime minister chooses which MPs serve as ministers. Senior ministers with the most responsibility form the **cabinet**, which meets weekly with the prime minister to discuss important issues facing the government. The prime minister and cabinet together are seen as responsible for the government. State and territory executive branches are organised in a similar way.

Separation of Powers

Even though the prime minister and ministers are members of the House of Representatives and the Senate, the **Constitution** states that the executive, **legislature** and the **judiciary** should act separately and independently from each other. Simply, the legislature makes the laws, the executive carries them out and the judiciary **interprets** them. This 'separation of powers' helps prevent one branch from becoming too strong and influencing the others too much.

Australia's Prime Ministers

Edmund Barton became Australia's first prime minister in 1901. Australia's longest serving prime minister was Robert Menzies, who spent more than 16 years in office.

Robert Menzies was Australia's longest serving prime minister.

Prime Ministers of Australia

Name	Party	Date Term Began	Date Term Ended
Edmund Barton	Protectionist	1 January 1901	24 September 1903
Alfred Deakin (1st time)	Protectionist	24 September 1903	27 April 1904
Chris Watson	Australian Labor Party	27 April 1904	18 August 1904
Sir George Reid	Free Trade	18 August 1904	5 July 1905
Alfred Deakin (2nd time)	Protectionist	5 July 1905	13 November 1908
Andrew Fisher (1st time)	Australian Labor Party	13 November 1908	2 June 1909
Alfred Deakin (3rd time)	Protectionist	2 June 1909	29 April 1910
Andrew Fisher (2nd time)	Australian Labor Party	29 April 1910	24 June 1913
Joseph Cook	Liberal Party of Australia	24 June 1913	17 September 1914
Andrew Fisher (3rd time)	Australian Labor Party	17 September 1914	27 October 1915
Billy Hughes	Australian Labor Party	27 October 1915	14 November 1916
Billy Hughes (2nd time)	Nationalist	14 November 1916	17 February 1917
Billy Hughes (3rd time)	Nationalist	17 February 1917	9 February 1923
Stanley Bruce	Nationalist	9 February 1923	22 October 1929
James Scullin	Australian Labor Party	22 October 1929	6 January 1932
Joseph Lyons	United Australia	6 January 1932	7 April 1939
Sir Earle Page	Australian Country	7 April 1939	26 April 1939
Robert Menzies (1st time)	United Australia	26 April 1939	28 August 1941
Arthur Fadden	Country	28 August 1941	7 October 1941
John Curtin	Australian Labor Party	7 October 1941	5 July 1945
Frank Forde	Australian Labor Party	6 July 1945	13 July 1945
Ben Chifley	Australian Labor Party	13 July 1945	19 December 1949
Sir Robert Menzies (2nd time)	Liberal	19 December 1949	6 January 1966
Harold Holt	Liberal	26 January 1966	19 December 1967
John McEwen	Country	19 December 1967	10 January 1968
John Gorton	Liberal	10 January 1968	10 March 1971
William McMahon	Liberal	10 March 1971	5 December 1972
Gough Whitlam	Australian Labor Party	5 December 1972	11 November 1975
Malcolm Fraser	Liberal	11 November 1975	11 March 1983
Bob Hawke	Australian Labor Party	11 March 1983	20 December 1991
Paul Keating	Australian Labor Party	20 December 1991	11 March 1996
John Howard	Liberal	11 March 1996	3 December 2007
Kevin Rudd	Australian Labor Party	3 December 2007	24 June 2010
Julia Gillard	Australia Labor Party	24 June 2010	Current

Cabinet

The word 'cabinet' comes from the French word meaning 'small room'. It was used to describe a small room where a king or queen's advisors regularly met. Eventually, the word came to describe the advisors, instead of the room.

Public Service

The public service is made up of people who work for the government. They provide the government with advice and help the government deliver its programs to the community. There are public servants for all levels of government: federal, state and local.

Government Departments

When the government says it is going to do something such as build a school, pave a road or provide help to people in need, someone has to do the actual work. Usually, people in government departments organise and carry out that work. These people are called 'public servants' because their work is to serve the community. Diplomats, federal police, national park rangers and customs officers are all examples of public servants.

Government departments are part of the **executive** branch. Unlike ministers, public servants are not elected. Public servants are hired to work in many kinds of jobs, and they carry out the instructions of whichever party is currently in power.

Organising Government Departments

Government departments are organised according to the work they do. The top public servant in a government department is called the departmental secretary, and he or she reports to the government minister in charge of the department. It is not unusual to have a minister overseeing more than one department or a department to have more than one minister.

Federal Government Departments

In 2011, there were 18 federal government departments. However, this number can change as the government changes how work is done. In the same way, ministers also change when the prime minister wants them to have different responsibilities or when a new party comes into power.

Centrelink is part of the Department of Human Services and provides a wide range of services, from delivering the government's family support programs to providing financial support for people facing hardship.

Federal Government Departments, 2011

Department	Responsible for ...
Agriculture, Fisheries and Forestry	• Agricultural, pastoral, fishing, food and forest industries • Water, soils, and other natural resources • Rural and drought issues • Rural industries inspection and quarantine
Attorney-General	• Providing advice and services to the government about law and justice, national security and human rights issues
Communications, Broadband and the Digital Economy	• Developing an effective broadband network • Promoting the digital economy • Information and communications technology • Post and telecommunications
Climate Change and Energy Efficiency	• Developing policy to combat climate change • Renewable energy targets • Reporting energy consumption and greenhouse gas emissions
Defence	• All defence-related activities
Education, Employment and Workplace Relations	• Education • Training • Workplace relations and policy • Ensuring that workplaces are safe and productive • Employment and related programs and services
Families, Housing, Community Services and Indigenous Affairs	• Supporting families with children, carers, and people in hardship • Supporting people with disabilities • Family relationship services • Services and programs for Indigenous Australians • Women's policies and programs
Finance and Deregulation	• Budget policy • Government financial accountability • Governance and financial management
Foreign Affairs and Trade	• Relations and communications with overseas governments • Treaties • Trade policy and promotion • Diplomatic and consular missions • International security
Health and Ageing	• Services for the aged • Public health and medical research • Health promotion and disease prevention • Health care of Aboriginal and Torres Strait Islander people • Drug abuse strategy • Regulating therapeutic goods
Human Services	• Child support • Centrelink • Medicare
Immigration and Citizenship	• Entry of people into Australia • Settlement of migrants and **refugees** • Promoting the benefits of citizenship and cultural diversity
Infrastructure and Transport	• Infrastructure policy • Transport policy • Airports and aviation • Transport security
Innovation, Industry, Science and Research	• Helping key industries grow • Promoting scientific research • Encouraging innovation • Developing policy to keep Australia competitive
Prime Minister and Cabinet	• Supporting the prime minister • Achieving a coordinated approach to developing and implementing government policies
Resources, Energy and Tourism	• Working with business to develop policy in resources, energy and tourism • Advising the government on resources, energy and tourism policy • Running clean energy programs
Sustainability, Environment, Water, Population and Communities	• Protecting the environment • Air quality • Fuel quality • Water policy • Environmental research • Housing affordability
Treasury	• Taxation • International finance • Foreign exchange • Finance policy • Currency

Judiciary

The **judiciary** is the third branch of government. It is up to the judiciary to **interpret** and apply laws through the court system.

Different Kinds of Courts

Australia has a number of different kinds of courts. Federal courts deal with questions about federal laws, while state and territory courts usually handle issues that come from state and territory laws. Therefore, a federal problem, such as something to do with banking or **immigration** law, would go to the federal court. A state problem, such as something to do with business regulation or traffic laws, would go to a state court.

The courts also have an order of importance. Most issues are initially tried in lower courts. If one of the people involved is unhappy with a court's decision, they **appeal** to a higher court to look at the case again. Appeals can go up to the highest court in Australia, the High Court, which has the final say over all laws and courts.

Judges and Independence

Judges in Australia are chosen by state, territory or federal government. Australian judges can stay in their jobs until they are 70 years old. Their jobs are safe even if there is a change of government. Judges can only be removed if they do something seriously wrong.

Judges' jobs are safe because of the separation of powers. Judges need to be able to interpret laws and make decisions without worrying that they may be removed if the government disagrees with the court's decisions. In fact, on occasion, judges may have to specifically say that something the government has done is wrong, or is against the **Constitution**, so the system needs to ensure that their jobs are safe.

The High Court of Australia hears cases dealing with constitutional issues. It is also Australia's highest court of appeal.

A new Chief Justice is sworn in at a ceremony at the Supreme Court of NSW in Sydney.

Australia's Courts

High Court of Australia

- Top court of appeal for both federal and state laws
- Judges constitutional issues

Federal Court of Australia

- Hears cases to do with trade, tax, social security, native title and **intellectual property**
- Hears appeals from Federal Magistrate Courts

Family Court of Australia

- Hears cases to do with family law, including marriage, divorce and child custody

State or Territory Supreme Court

- Top court of appeal for the state or territory

Federal Magistrate Courts

- Hears simpler cases that would otherwise go to either the Federal or Family Court

District Court (called County Court in some states)

- Hears criminal trials and most matters between private individuals

Magistrate's Court (called Local Court in some states)

- Hears simpler and less severe cases, including those that do not need a jury

Influencing the Government

The process of trying to influence government decisions is called lobbying. It is usually practised by people with a special interest. That special interest might be a type of business, a cause such as conservation or development, or a particular type of medical research.

Who Lobbies the Government?

Australia has millions of people with many different ideas and interests. It is almost impossible for a government to make a decision that makes everyone happy. For example, if a forest is protected, conservationists are happy but loggers might be angry. The opposite decision will have the opposite result.

Businesses and special-interest groups often try to influence the government to make decisions and create policies that they agree with or that they think will benefit them in some way. They do this by making their views known to politicians and by using whatever influence they can.

Effective Lobby Groups

Some of most effective lobby groups have a large number of people associated with them with a narrow set of interests. If politicians think a lot of people support something, they are more likely to make a decision that benefits that group. Groups such as Greenpeace, Amnesty International and the National Farmers Federation all make constant efforts to influence politicians.

Professional Lobbyists

Lobbying is a skill. Professional lobbyists make lobbying their job, and learn how to do it very well. They are hired by organisations that want their views heard.

Successful Lobbying

Who to Lobby?

There is no point talking to the wrong person. You have to talk to someone who can affect the outcome. Decide if you have a local, state or federal issue, work out who can make the decision, then approach him or her.

How to Lobby?

There are lots of ways to lobby, but some work better than others. One of the best is meeting someone in person. A careful, calm and well-planned conversation is a great way to get a point across. Phone calls, letters, emails and petitions can also be effective.

Petitions

A petition involves a lot of people signing a request asking the government to do something, such as protecting a forest or stopping inappropriate development in a town. Getting a lot of signatures is a way of showing the government that there is a lot of support for the issue.

Protests are a form of lobbying. These people successfully lobbied the government to protect the Franklin River in Tasmania in 1983.

Lobbying

The term 'lobbying' dates back to the 1830s and comes from the United States. People who wanted to influence federal or state government waited around in lobbies (the front part of building) to try to speak with politicians when they came out of their chambers. The term now applies to all forms of trying to influence the government.

Voters can speak to their local House of Representatives MP about issues that concern them.

Timeline

1890
The Australian Labor Party is established.

1901
The colonies federate to form a new level of government known as the federal government.

Australia's first federal elections are held.

Federal Parliament meets for the first time, in Melbourne.

1902
Most men and women over 21 can vote in federal elections.

Women are given the vote in New South Wales.

1903
Women are given the vote in Tasmania.

The High Court of Australia is established by the **Judiciary** Act.

1905
Electoral subdivisions are created.

Women are given the vote in Queensland.

1906
Postal voting is made available for the first time.

1908
Women are given the vote in Victoria.

1913

The Country Party (later to become the National Party) is established in Western Australia.

1919
Preferential voting is first used in a federal election.

1924
Compulsory voting is introduced for federal elections.

1927
Parliament meets in Canberra for the first time, on 9 May.

1944
The Liberal Party of Australia is established.

1949
Indigenous Australians are given the right to vote at federal elections if they are entitled to vote in their state elections (NSW, South Australia, Victoria, Tasmania) or have served in the Defence Forces.

1962
Voting at federal elections is extended to all Indigenous Australians.

1967
A regerendum changes the Constitution to allow Indigenous people to be counted in the Australian population.

1973
The age for enrolment and voting in federal elections is lowered from 21 years to 18 years.

1984

Compulsory enrolment and voting is introduced for Indigenous Australians.

1992
The Australian Greens Party is established.

2001
A Virtual Tally Room (VTR) is developed for the Australian Electoral Commission website to provide up-to-the-minute results on election night.

2007
Electronic voting trials are conducted at the federal election for vision impaired people.

Remote electronic voting trials are conducted for certain Australian Defence Force personnel serving overseas.

Glossary

abbreviation shortened version of a word or name

administrator person who works as the manager in government, business or education

appeal ask a higher court to review a lower court's decision

armed forces military—army, navy and air force

assembly gathering of citizens

balance of power ability to direct an outcome by casting a vote one way or another

ballot act of voting; paper used to vote

bicameral parliament that has two separate chambers

cabinet committee of senior ministers

ceremonial to do with ceremonies, rituals and formal occasions

citizenship legal right to belong to a country

coalition two or more political parties grouping together to form one block

commonwealth group of states or nations with common interests

compulsory voting system that requires eligible voters to vote in elections

constitution document that outlines how a country is to be governed, the structure of its government, and the rights and protections the country will give to its citizens

democracy system of government in which representatives are chosen by the people through elections

dictatorship government where one person has absolute power and makes decisions without being restrained by laws

eligible someone who is fit and entitled to be chosen for something

executive part of government that leads and makes decisions

electorate area containing a certain number of people who are represented by a member of parliament

financial to do with money and finances

Governor-General person who acts as head of state of Australia on behalf of the British king or queen

immigration when someone goes to live in another country where they were not born

intellectual property creative work that is owned by the person who created it

interpret decide what is meant by something

judiciary part of government that upholds and interprets the law through the court system

legislature part of government that has the power to make laws

mayor person who is the head of a local government

military junta military officers who seize power and rule a country by force

monarch king or queen

money bill law that has to do with the government collecting or spending money

native title law that recognises that there is and has been continuous land ownership of Australian land by Australia's Indigenous people

parliament assembly of citizens elected to represent the people

policies guidelines and plans created by governments that deal with particular issues, such as immigration or health

preferential voting voting for every candidate on the ballot paper in order of preference

proportional voting system of electing representatives to parliment in proportion to the number of votes they recieve

quarantine isolation of goods and animals before they enter a country to make sure they do not carry any diseases

refugee person who seeks protection from war or other dangers in another country

representative person chosen to represent others

seat refers to the 'seat' or position in parliament each member of parliament holds

sewerage system of pipes used to remove waste

theocracy government ruled by religious leaders

Index